Aircraft
Adults Coloring Book

Anthony Hutzler

Sketch Coloring Book

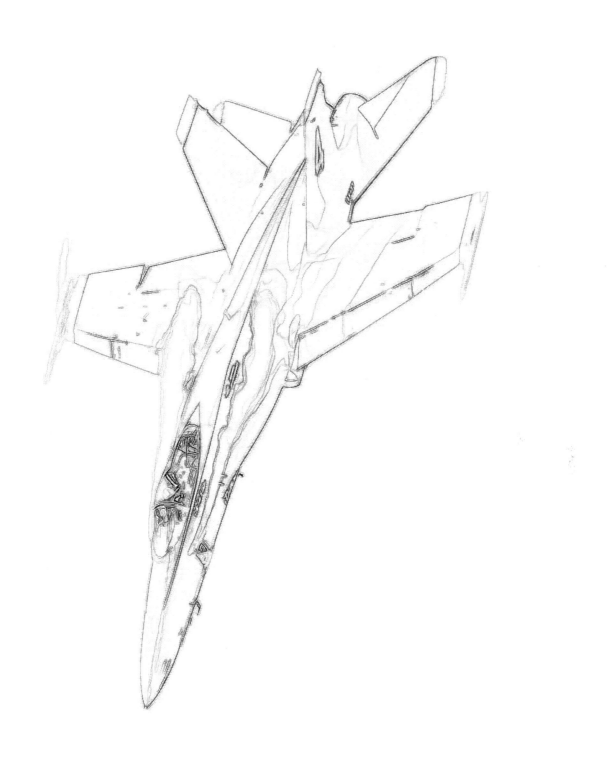

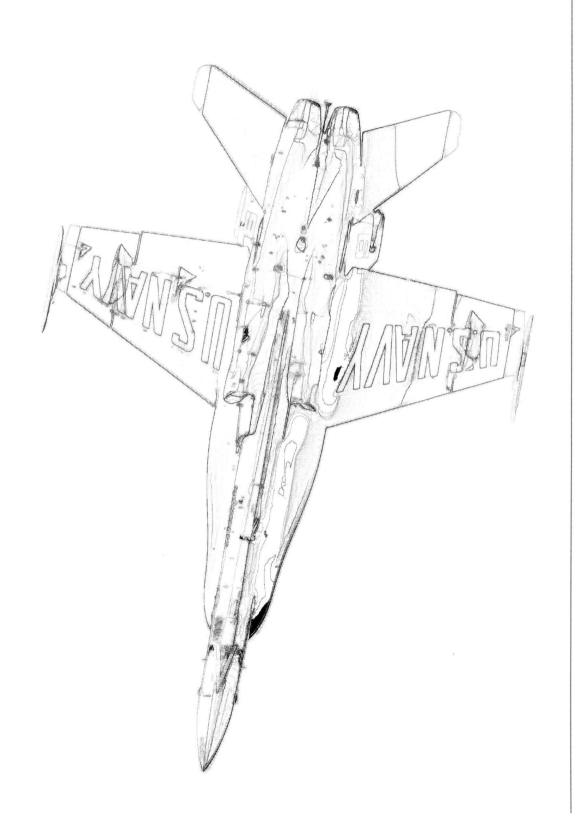

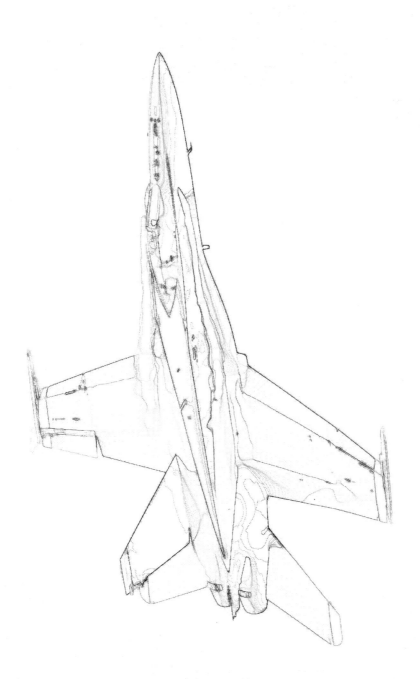

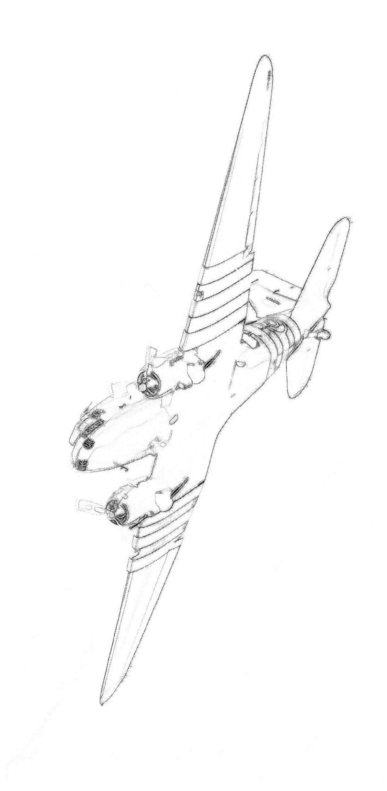

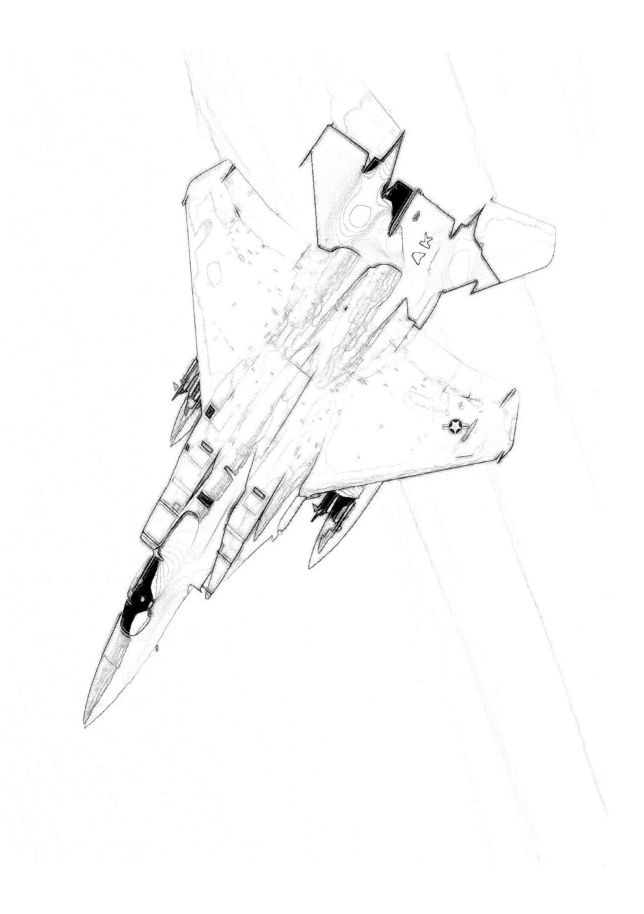

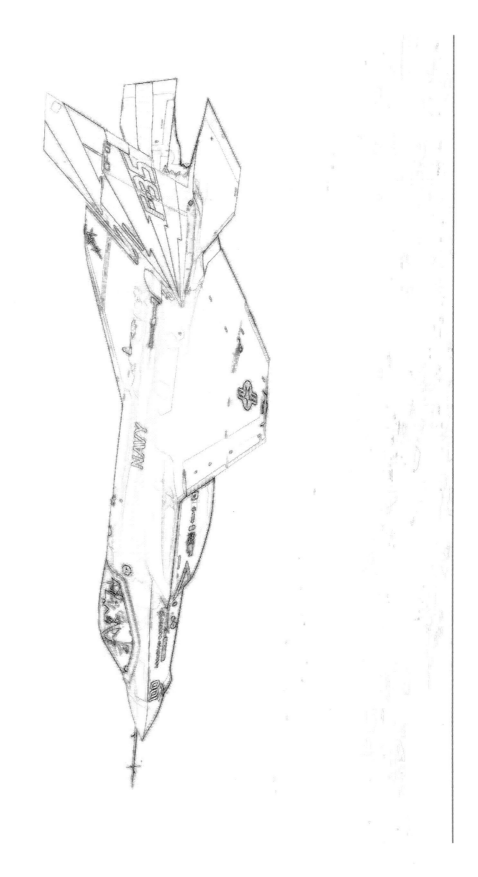

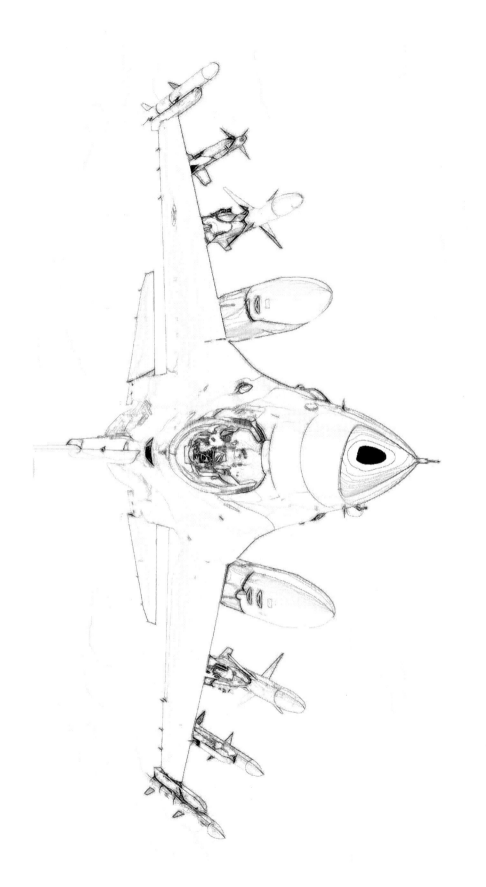

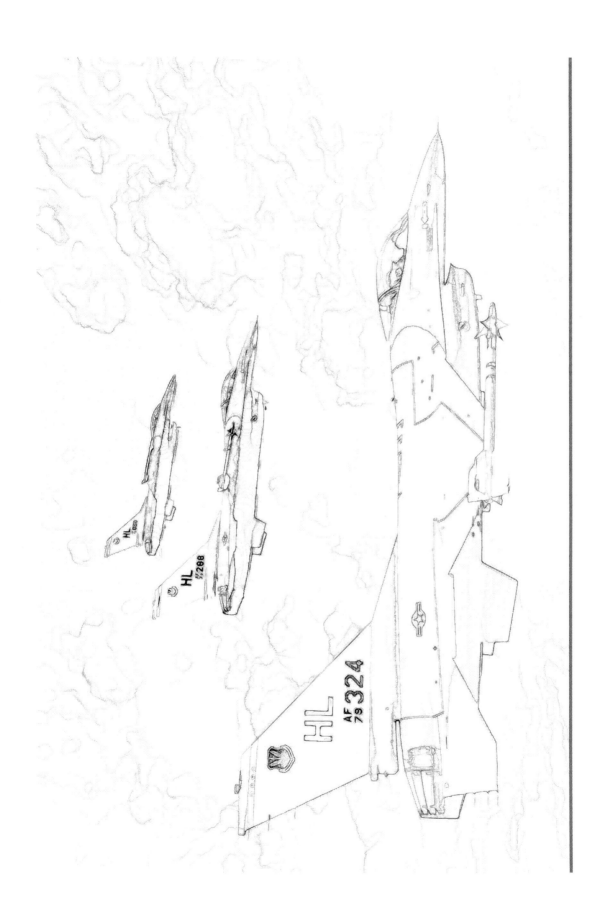

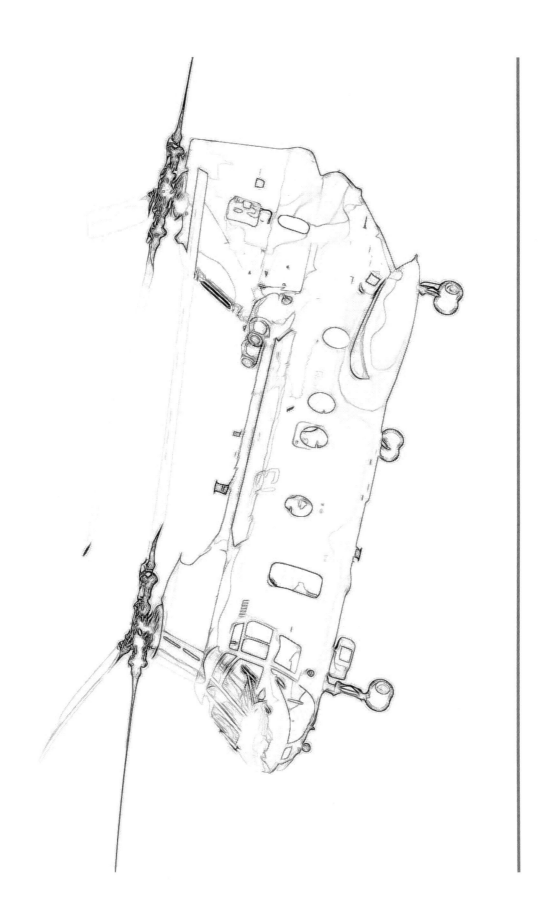

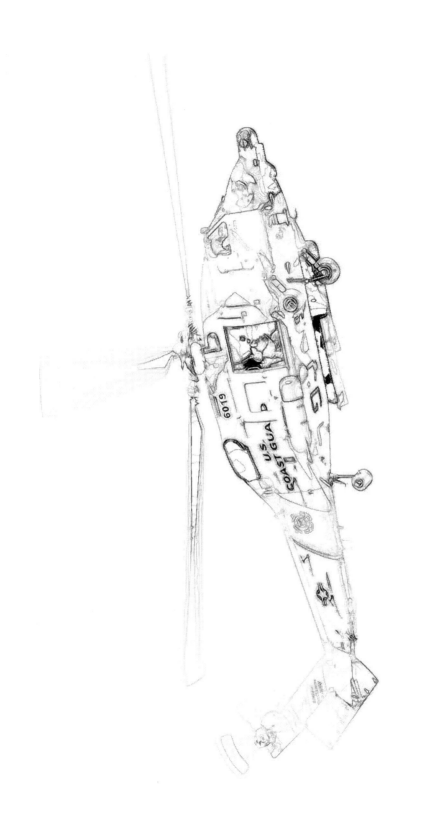

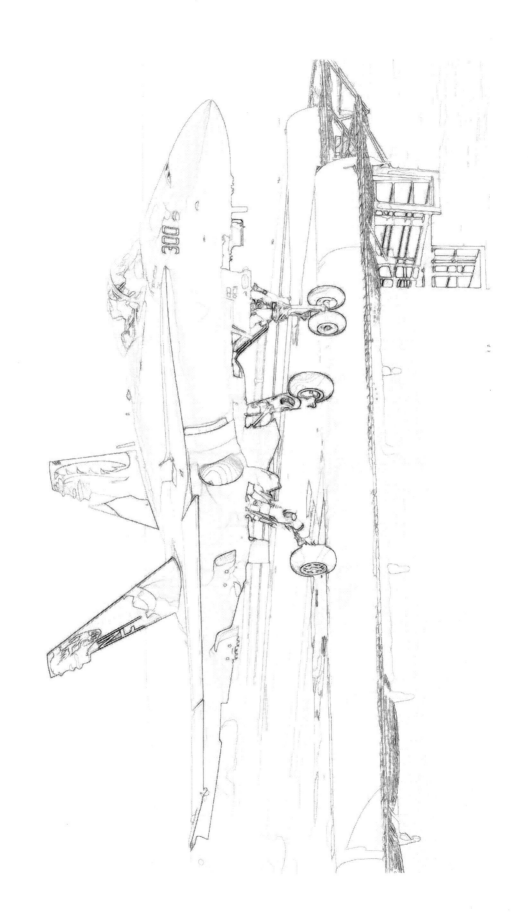

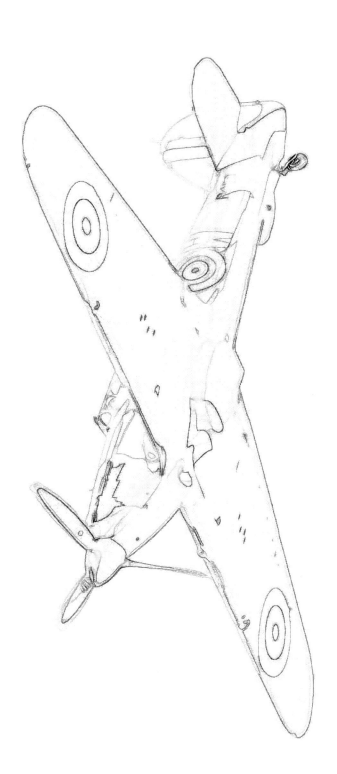

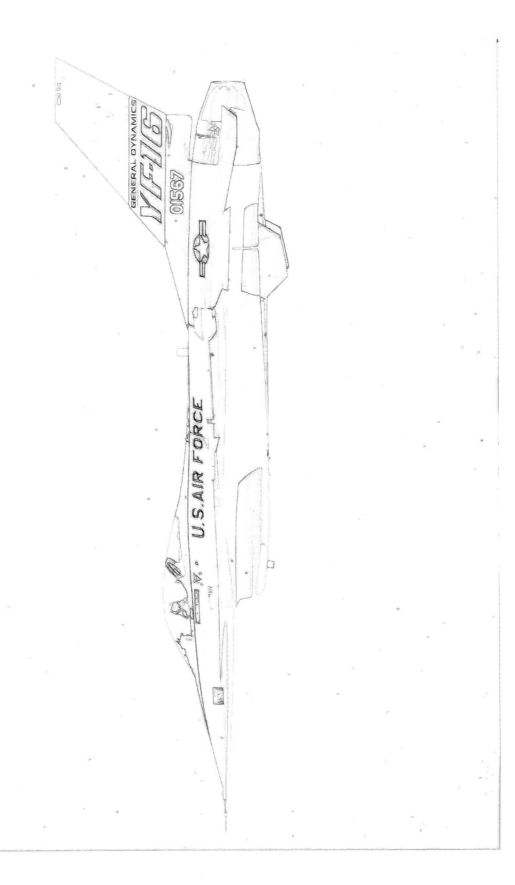

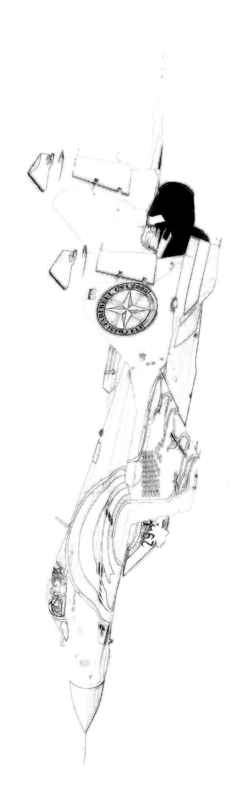

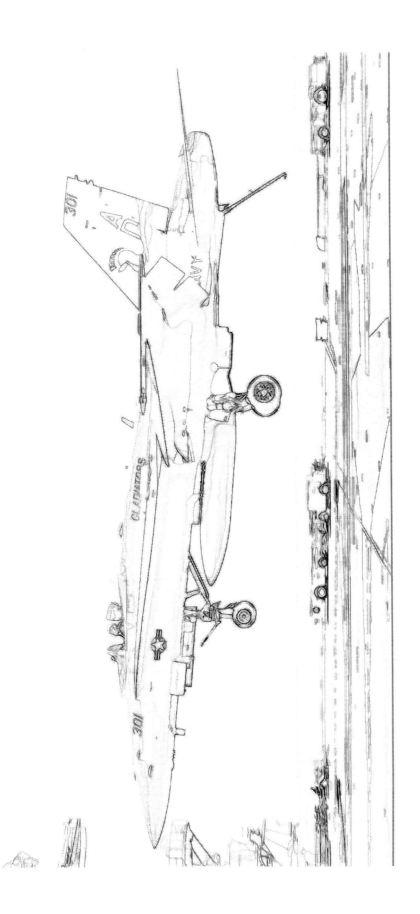

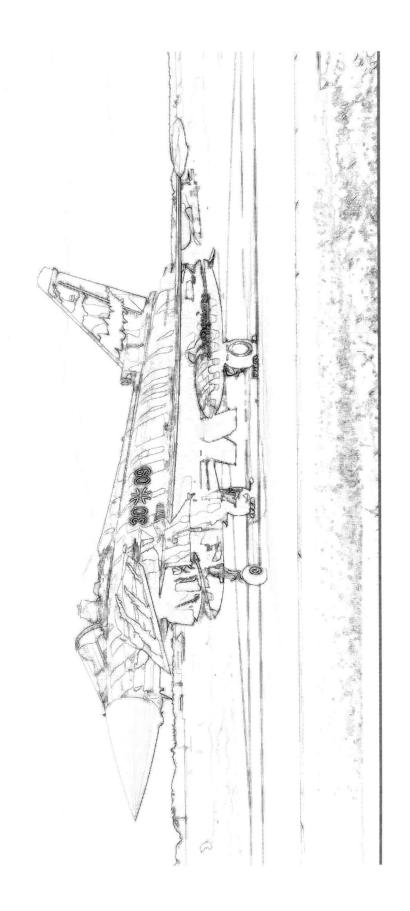

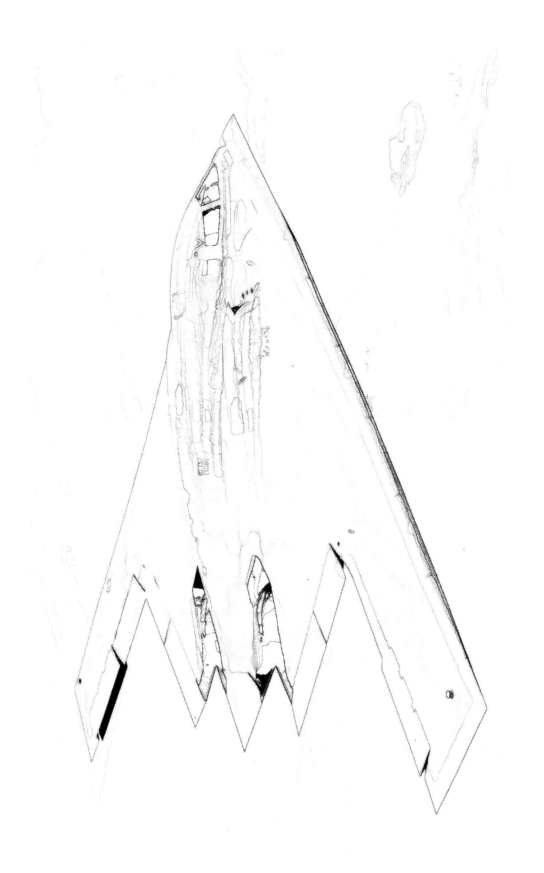

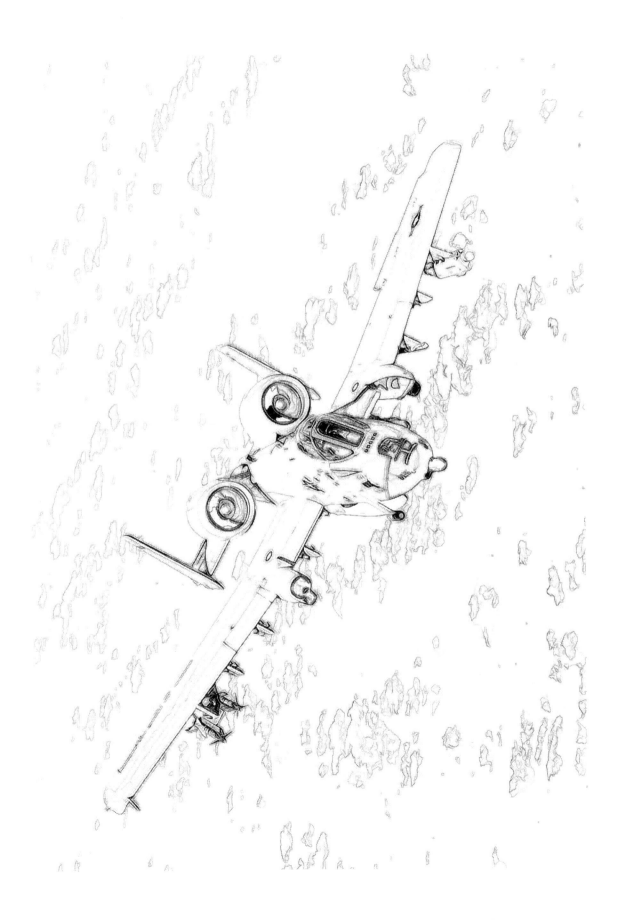

Original Photo : http://bit.ly/2cpHNu3
PDF file : http://bit.ly/2bYdI5z

http://bit.ly/good_vibes_1

ISBN : 1530381223
(Use this ISBN for searching on amazon.com)

Made in the USA
Middletown, DE
10 July 2018